Six Weeks to a

BRAIN UPGRADE

A Student's Quick-Start Guide for Using Brain Research to Boost Learning

Janet Nay Zadina, Ph.D.

Order at <u>www.brainresearch.us</u>

Dear Student,

This book could change your life. Scientists have discovered that you can change your brain and you can become more intelligent. This book is going to show you how. With only 30 brief tips you will learn how to be smarter, not just get a better grade. You can make important changes to your brain.

I was a teacher before I became a cognitive neuroscientist specializing in Educational Neuroscience. This enables me to find, read, and understand the latest research about how we learn and how to make learning stronger and easier. It also enables me to understand what this means about what learners need to do in the classroom and how hard it is for some students to do well. I am not going to bore you with long explanations of "study skills." No, we are going to take a "get it done" approach. I tell you what the scientists have discovered and what it can mean to you. Then I give you an important tip called *Just Do This*.

Here is a chance for you to make a big difference in your learning and your life skills. Please read about the research and then try out the tips from the "brain doctor" and see what happens. You can take charge of your brain! Start now! Just do it!

Sincerely yours,
Dr. Janet Zadina

Contents

Plasticity

The brain you have today is not the one you were born with. From the moment you took your first breath, your brain began shaping itself especially for your particular environment. As a human being, your brain possesses more uncommitted cortex than any other species on earth. That gives you an extraordinary capacity for learning. In the presence of an enriched environment, your brain continuously grows new and faster connections. The more connections you grow, the smarter you become. The ability of your brain to change physically in response to learning is called **plasticity**.

How Neurons Connect

When people talk about "gray matter" they are referring to brain cells, or **neurons**. You have at least a hundred billion of them and they work full time transmitting information. The process begins when neurons receive information through their branches, or **dendrites**. If enough signals arrive through the dendrites to stimulate the neuron, it will fire, meaning that it sends the information in the form of electrical pulses down its **axon**. At the end of the axon is a gap, called a **synapse**. The tip of the

The key to getting smarter is to make new synaptic connections!

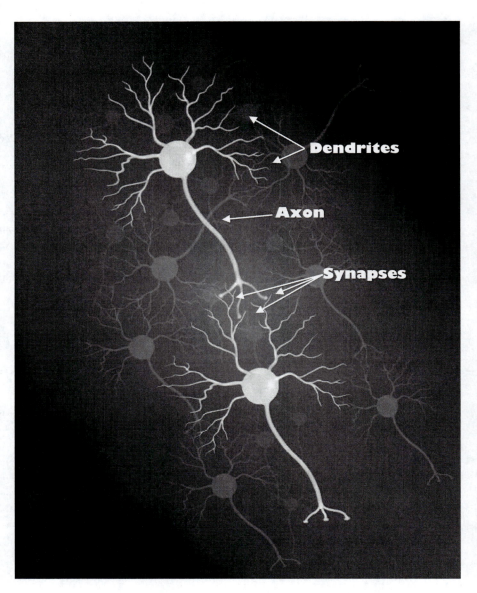

axon releases chemicals, called **neurotransmitters**, which carry the information across the synapse to the dendrites of the next neuron. We refer to this process as **firing**.

Transmission

A well-traveled axon is covered in a casing made of a type of white matter, or glia, called myelin. Composed of 80% fat and 20% protein, this myelin sheath increases the speed at which messages travel to the next neuron. A well-myelinated axon results in faster transmission. Damaged or destroyed myelin can result in diseases like multiple sclerosis and Guillain-Barré syndrome.

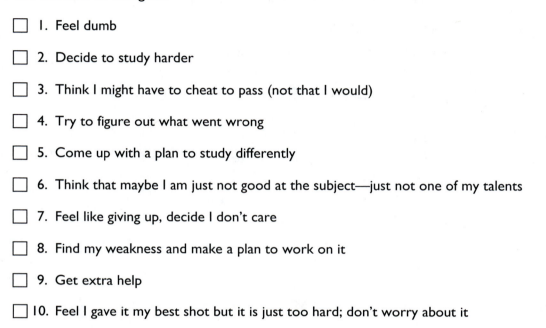

A.1—Mindset

How do you react when you get a paper back with a low grade? Think about the last low score you got and try to recall your feelings. Check all the boxes that apply. Be very honest, as this is so that you can look inside your own brain and find out how to change it.

☐ 1. Feel dumb

☐ 2. Decide to study harder

☐ 3. Think I might have to cheat to pass (not that I would)

☐ 4. Try to figure out what went wrong

☐ 5. Come up with a plan to study differently

☐ 6. Think that maybe I am just not good at the subject—just not one of my talents

☐ 7. Feel like giving up, decide I don't care

☐ 8. Find my weakness and make a plan to work on it

☐ 9. Get extra help

☐ 10. Feel I gave it my best shot but it is just too hard; don't worry about it

In boxes A and B below, circle the number of the items that you checked. For example, if you put a check mark beside Item 3 above, then you would circle the number 3 below.

A					B				
1	3	6	7	10	2	4	5	8	9

Now let's see what this may mean.

If you circled more items in box A than Box B, you might have a *fixed* mindset (you will learn about this). Read those items again and think how this attitude could lead to defeat. What if someone joined a gym and started lifting weights and had this attitude?

Congratulations if you have more circles in Box B. You realize that you can grow your brain and improve your grades. Reread the items in Box B. This is a *growth* mindset. This is an attitude that leads to success.

If you had more items in Box A, then reread the items listed in Box B and make a deliberate effort to change your mind to this attitude—the kind of attitude successful people have. You **can** change your mind! Change your mind, change your life!

FIRE IT

A.2—How in Charge Are You?

Write the number in the blank that best describes how you **usually** behave.
Answer **honestly** so you can find out how to improve your brain.

5) always   4) most of the time   3) maybe   2) not very often   1) never

_____   1.   I control my anxiety or nervousness on tests.

_____   2.   I believe that I can succeed in this course if I work hard enough.

_____   3.   I believe that hard work is more important than natural talent at something.

_____   4.   I am able to control distracting or upsetting thoughts.

_____   5.   I draw pictures to help me remember.

_____   6.   I ask myself questions about the material before and while I read.

_____   7.   I believe that you can change the IQ (intelligence) you were born with.

_____   8.   I test myself on the material.

_____   9.   I think of how what I already know relates to the material that is new.

_____   10. I look up information to understand new material better.

_____   11. I think about how well I understand material and back up if necessary.

_____   12. I make notes on what I don't understand and get it explained.

_____   13. I plan my schedule for doing assignments in a planner.

_____   14. I am organized.

_____   15. I control my emotions.

_____   16. I study my wrong answers to figure out why I missed them.

_____   17. I have a system for taking notes.

_____   18. I have several ways to make information easier to remember.

_____   19. I can control my attention in class.

_____   20. I get 8 hours of sleep a night and/or I take naps.

_____   21. I avoid studying right before a test.

_____   22. I use more than one sense when learning: seeing, hearing, speaking, or writing.

_____   23. I study with other students outside of class.

_____   24. I turn assignments in on time.

_____   25. I am happy with the grades that I have been making.

How are you doing now? Add your points and check your score:

100+   You are doing well! Improve where you can and help other students. You will get even better!

51–99   You will benefit greatly from doing the activities in this book. Do all of them, add new habits, and experience better learning!

0–50   You **can** change your brain and raise this score. Devote yourself wholeheartedly to this book. Keep doing all the new strategies that you learn, adding to your skills and habits. Watch other students and learn from their skills. You will make progress and see results!

FIRE IT

A.3—What is Intelligence?

1. IQ is a term that refers to tests that claim to measure someone's intelligence. What is intelligence?

   _____

   _____

2. Why do some people have a higher IQ than others?

   _____

   _____

3. Which characteristics do you think would be associated with people with a higher IQ?

   ☐ Read more

   ☐ Ask questions

   ☐ Work hard

   ☐ Born smart

4. One of those characteristics is *no longer* believed to be true. Cross it out.

A.4—What Will It Take?

Max M. Ize wants to have a great body by the time summer comes. He decides to join a gym and thinks that a few visits might do it, so he gets a one-month membership. How would you advise him? How many "reps" (repetitions of an action) would it take to go from lifting a 10-pound weight to his goal of 50 pounds?

_____

_____

_____

The Research

Thinking involves communication within the brain. Just as when you communicate with other people you exchange information, when the brain thinks, the brain cells (*neurons*) exchange information. The information that you know is stored in your neurons, often called *gray matter*. This information is stored in the form of chemicals.

> There is a difference between thinking and learning!

How does this exchange work? Just as any system that communicates must have an input (we have ears) and an output (we have a mouth). The neurons output is called an axon and the input is a dendrite. To communicate (think), the chemicals are transmitted from the axon of one neuron into the dendrites of other neurons, but they don't touch each other. Instead, electrical impulses fire the chemicals across a gap (synapse) between the axon and the dendrite.

In order to think about something, tens of thousands of neurons related to the topic will communicate at the same time. We call this a neural network. If you think of the word "table" you can picture many kinds of tables or the verb table) and your network of information on "table" is firing together. Neurons in many parts of the brain are making connections and firing in this neural network.

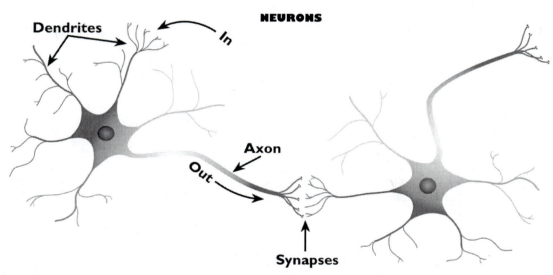

So What?

In this book, we will refer to thinking as firing a network. So before you can learn anything, you must fire up an existing neural network in the brain. Sometimes it is effortful to think about something because these neurons are so tiny that they must make connections across huge (to them) distances in the brain. Sometimes they have a hard time finding the information, as when you have trouble remembering something. Once this network is activated (fired) by your thinking, it disappears—unless you have created a pathway or strong neural network through learning (lesson 2).

Just Do This!

Study the next page carefully about how the brain learns so you can learn the difference between thinking and real learning. Then you can ask yourself when you are in class or studying, am I just thinking, or am I learning?

Reflect and Connect:

How can this information make a difference to you?

The Research:

Neuroscientists (brain scientists) have a saying called the Hebbian Law—the "law" of how learning occurs in the brain: *Cells that fire together, wire together.* When a group of neurons fire together, they are more likely to fire together again. That is how learning takes place: fire it until you wire it. The scientific name for this is long-term potentiation (LTP). You say the same thing when you say "practice makes perfect" or "practice makes permanent."

Fire it until you wire it!

The brain is like a muscle in many ways:

1. The more you use it, the stronger it gets.
2. The more you work on parts of it, the bigger those parts get.
3. The more you work on it, the more it can do.
4. The kinds of things you do with it affect the results that you get.

As we go through this book, you will use this metaphor of the brain as a muscle and of a bodybuilder trying to create a better body. This metaphor will help you understand the brain better and to remember the information.

Instead of growing muscle tissue, when you learn your brain grows brain tissue in the form of dendrites. The more you learn, the more dendrites you grow. These dendrites create connections between neurons, creating a *neural network*: a group of neurons that fire together. When you think, you fire a network, but when you learn, you *wire* a network, meaning that you have made a lasting connection between neurons that will enable them to fire together again. If you fire this network enough, then when you want to remember it, you will be able to fire it—to recreate the network in your brain—and to remember it for a test.

So it isn't enough to fire it, you have to wire it! That means that you have to keep firing it over and over—repetition—to make it stronger. So one of the most important factors in learning is repetition.

So What?

Learning is effortful—it takes a great deal of effort! Yes, it is hard and sometimes frustrating and discouraging. Think about the TV show *Dancing with the Stars*. What do the dancers do when they get a low score? They don't give up; they take advice and say that they will work harder because they know that learning something new is hard work. They do lots of repetition of the dance moves so that these moves will be recalled when they perform. This is how people learn.

In order to succeed in school, you must repeat the information that you want to learn until you can recall it. You must fire it until you wire it! You must keep activating the network so that you can activate it later—remember.

Once you realize that everyone has to work hard when they learn something new, you can just go ahead and put the hard work into it. In the next lesson, you will learn why it might *seem* that some people don't have to work hard.

Just Do This!

Repeat material until you know it to grow new dendrites and keep them!

Reflect and Connect:

How hard have you worked when you studied compared to how hard someone would work in a gym to build muscle? What will you do differently now?

The Research:

About 25 years ago scientists made an amazing discovery! They found out that people can change their brains and raise their IQ (intelligence). Prior to that, they thought everyone had the brain they were born with and some were born smart and some weren't. Now we know that you can control how smart you are! You can do things that change your brain.

> You can do things that raise your IQ!

Researcher Bogdan Draganski used brain scan machines to look inside the brains of medical students. Those who studied showed changes in two important brain areas. They had more gray matter! They had changed their brains by studying. Dr. Marcel Just says that we are not at the mercy of our biology, meaning we can improve what we have now. We can take control.

Several important research studies have shown that when students who were not doing well in school learned that they could change their brains, their grades started improving, while those who didn't know that continued to get poor grades. Why? Because once you know that you can change your brain, you will work harder in school knowing that you are working to become smarter.

So What?

This means that you can change your brain and raise your intelligence. You can do things that will make you a smarter person and make your brain better. For example, if you were not good at math in the past, you can strengthen those neural networks and get better at math. How? By doing math! By finding out where the gaps are in what you already know and filling them in by learning the information you may have missed.

The harder it is, the more you struggle, the better for your brain, just like working out hard in the gym. Lifting light weights doesn't make much of a difference, does it? Give your brain a good hard workout by trying everything in this book. Then think about what is happening in your brain. If you and your friends joined a gym, some would be able to start with heavier weights than others. You might have to start with lighter weights because you have to build up your muscles to where they are actually starting. That is not because they were born stronger; it is because they made themselves stronger throughout life by using their muscles more than you did. So they have an advantage when they start the first day in the gym. But that doesn't mean you can't catch up or even pass them up; it just might take you more time.

For subjects that you really struggle with, get help and work on those weak neural networks. There is nothing to get discouraged about. Practice, practice, practice. The more you do, the better at it you get. This changes your brain. You have grown new neural networks.

Just Do This!

Work hard at the activities in this book. Think about what works for you and what doesn't. Then add what works.

Reflect and Connect:

What does this information mean to you? How will it affect your behavior?

The Research:

James Zull is a cell biologist at Case Western University in Ohio. He says that the single most important factor in learning is the student's existing neural network. He means the existing knowledge on the topic that the learner already has before learning new material. The student who struggles with new material may have some gaps in their neural network—may be missing some important information that other students already knew.

> *You can't wire it if you can't even fire it.*

So What?

You can't "wire" new information if you can't even "fire" it—if you can't connect new information to existing information in your brain. The most important first step is to make a connection from what is in your brain to new information. Sometimes things seem to come easier to other students. This is probably because they have more experience on the topics—stronger neural networks. You may have to fill in some gaps before you can begin to learn new material. If new material seems confusing or too difficult, you may need to back up a step and get some additional information or practice to fill in the gap.

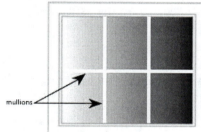

mullions

It is important to put information in context—in a bigger picture—to make it part of your neural network. For example, you might not know the word mullions, but if I said "when you paint the windows, use a very tiny paintbrush to paint all the mullions that run up and down and across; tape off the small sections of glass so you do not get paint on them," you might guess what mullions are. But if you have never seen them, and have no neural network on mullions, that might not be enough. However, a quick look at Google Image and you can then figure it out.

It is always a good idea to get a basic overview before learning new content. This allows you to understand the overview and then connect the more difficult new information to that. It also helps fill in any gaps or refresh your memory. Here are some easy ways.

1. Search on YouTube. You can find demonstrations and explanations of almost anything.
2. Do an Internet search on key words or topics. Use chapter headings or subheadings in the chapter to get ideas for search terms. Then read some of the simpler versions that you find.
3. If you are struggling with math, science, or economics go to www.khanacademy.org where you can find free simple explanations that have helped thousands of students. There are over 2,000 videos made for students.
4. Go to Wikipedia for an overview. Wikipedia, along with other Internet sites, may not be as accurate as your classroom materials, but they are helpful at getting an overview and firing up your networks.
5. Use Google Image to find pictures of vocabulary terms. Pictures can be more helpful than definitions.

Just Do This!

Before you start a new unit, find ways to connect to the new material. Ask yourself:

1. What do I already know about this? Make notes on that.
2. Ask yourself whether you need to refresh your memory or get some more information before starting the unit or while working on the unit.

Reflect and Connect:

What does it mean "you can't wire it if you can't even fire it"? Give an example of a time when you didn't understand something because you were missing important background information.

Research

Mindset: Researcher Carol Dweck found one important difference between people who were more successful and those who were not as successful. She called this difference *mindset*. Unsuccessful people had a mindset (attitude set in their minds) that was *fixed*: you were either born smart or talented or not. Successful people, on the other hand, knew that you create your own smarts: you get smarter by working at it—a *growth* mindset. Successful people knew that talent and skills are something that get better with practice. Some people may seem to have an advantage, may seem to be born with a natural talent or smarts, but others surpass them by getting better as time goes on.

> You can change your mindset and become more successful!

Belief: Brain scans show that when someone's brain *believes* that they can do something successfully, the brain puts forth more neural effort—the brain tries harder! Cognitive psychologist Jennifer Mangels suggests that beliefs affect learning success because the brain focuses attention and thinking toward information that helps achieve goals.

Intention: When you *intend* to do something, you are sending a message to the brain. *Intention drives attention.* You pay more attention if you *intend* to learn or intend to do something. One research study showed that when students are given an assignment, if they write down when and where they *intend* to do the assignment, they are more likely to do it. Apparently the brain is listening to your thoughts.

So What?

While the brain controls many functions, **you**, your mind, controls your brain in many ways. You can control your mindset, your beliefs, your intentions, your attitude, and your response to events.

Mindset: While your mindset may have been unconscious (without choosing it deliberately or thinking about it) you now have a **choice** of attitude. You can change your mindset and become more successful. You have learned that you can change your brain through activities. You will learn more about that throughout this workbook. Now that you know you can grow your brain in a desired direction, you can change your mindset from *fixed* (that's just how I am) to *growth* (with practice and experience I can get better).

Belief; What are you telling your brain? If your self-talk includes thoughts such as "I'll never be able to do this," "I'm just not good at this," or "I can't," then you are programming your brain to fail.

Intention: Set intentions. Most people know that writing down goals and to-do lists of things they *intend* to do make it more likely they will do them. Use this powerful tool.

Just Do This!

Change your mindset. Think in terms of growth and progress over time. Be aware of your beliefs and inner self-talk. Change it to something that works for you, not against you. When you are given an assignment, as you write down the assignment, write down when and where you intend to do it. In the back of this book is a form that you can use to write down your assignments. Begin today writing all assignments on that form. Be sure to use the *when* and *where* columns. Start today making lists of things you need to do and checking them off. Write your big goals in the front of your notebook or on a sticky note on your mirror. Focus on where you want to go and you will get there.

The hardest part of this book may be for you to change how you see yourself—your mindset, attitudes, and beliefs. But that could be the most important thing you do for yourself, affecting every aspect of your life and your future.

Reflect and Connect:

How have your current mindset, beliefs, and intentions been working for you? What changes will you make?

1. Look at the following illustration and see if you can figure out the difference between *information* and *knowledge* based on what you learned in this chapter. Write your explanation here.

_____

_____

_____

_____

_____

INFORMATION	KNOWLEDGE

2. Use a current reading assignment that you have not yet started. Glance through the assignment and look at any headings, subheadings, or illustrations. Look at the questions or problems. Write down what you already know on the subject or anything you can think of that might relate to the material. Do this on a full sheet of paper. Keep this paper in your notebook and use it to study.

3. a. Give examples of some things that you know you have a large, strong neural network on. This would be something that you know a lot about or are good at. For example, if you went camping often growing up, you could write down many things that you would know, such as how to build a fire, how to set up a tent, how to prepare food outside. What aspect of camping were you especially good at? Could you identify many trees or birds as you hiked? If you lived in a city, you might have a strong network on how to get around on a subway, train, or bus as a result of years of experience. Draw a line down the middle of the paper from top to bottom. On the left side, list as many as you can on a sheet of paper titled *Strong and Weak Neural Networks*.

b. Now on the right hand side, list some things that you are **not yet** good at, things you have not yet developed a strong neural network for. For example, if you are currently taking a gym class that requires you to play soccer and you have never played soccer, then you know you will not have as strong a neural network as the others in the class who have played soccer.

c. At the bottom of the sheet, write a reflection on the difference between the two lists. Why do you have strong networks on some things and not others? What are the differences between the lists?

d. Conclude this activity with a statement about how you could move items from the right side to the left—how you could end the year with strong neural networks on the items that are currently weak.

4. On another sheet of paper, describe some time that you doubted yourself but discovered you could succeed after all. This could be any activity or behavior: sports, church or club activity, family life, household tasks or repairs, or something at school.

5. What is one thing that you are really good at? _____

Were you born with this (a natural) or did you *become* good at it? Explain:

_____

_____

_____

_____

6. Before you read this chapter did you have a *fixed* or *growth* mindset? _____

How would you describe your mindset now? _____

Describe your current attitude toward your intelligence, talents, and abilities as a result of reading this chapter:

_____

_____

_____

_____

_____

FIRE IT

1. List your five senses
   a. _____
   b. _____
   c. _____
   d. _____
   e. _____

2. For each sense, list how you use that sense when you are studying:
   a. _____
   b. _____
   c. _____
   d. _____
   e. _____

3. Finish this saying: "A picture is worth _____."

4. Using several sentences, explain what this means. _____
   _____
   _____

5. How could you apply this to learning? _____
   _____

6. In a few sentences, explain how you organize items in your kitchen cabinet. _____
   _____
   _____

7. Why do you do that, and how could this apply to learning? _____
   _____

8. What is the purpose of taking notes in class? _____
   _____

9. What are your special tricks and strategies for taking notes? _____
   _____

10. Do you ever know something, but can't say it? Why do you think this happens? _____
    _____
    _____

11. What could you do to correct the problem in #10?
    _____
    _____

Activate multiple pathways for stronger learning!

The Research

Scientists know that the more pathways by which you take in information, the stronger the memory. Using more senses is called *multisensory experience* and involves more parts of the brain.

While the brain is very interconnected, certain parts of the brain have specialties. The brain has four major sections, called *lobes*. Vision is processed in the *occipital* lobe, near the back of your head. What you hear is processed in the *temporal* lobe, behind your ears. Speaking and writing involve movement—motor skills—and are processed in the *sensory motor strip* in the *parietal* lobe, near the top of your head. The fourth lobe, *frontal* lobe, is located behind your forehead. You will learn more about this in Week Four.

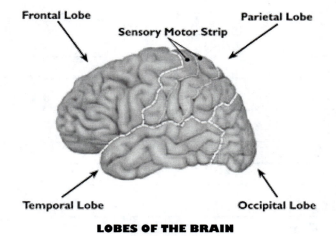

LOBES OF THE BRAIN

Each of these lobes has pathways to other lobes. If you see words while you are listening to them, you are getting more activation in the occipital lobe as well as in the temporal lobe. If you say it or write it down, you are getting more activation in the parietal lobe. And if you *think* carefully about what you are reading or writing, you are getting activation in the frontal lobe.

The more pathways you can involve, the larger and stronger the network. Scientist Richard Mayer tested learners and found that the groups getting multisensory input remembered the material much better and the memory lasted longer—even up to 20 years! Research suggests that the more you elaborate on the material (using it in different ways and thinking more about it), the better the learning. Also, if you Fire more pathways, and you can't access one of them well on the test, you may be able to access another pathway to recall the information.

So What?

I am sure it makes sense to you that if you use more than one sense—pathway—you would have a stronger memory based on what you learned in Week One. You know that you need to create strong neural networks and using more parts of your brain creates a larger network. If you can't remember what you *saw*, maybe you can think about what you *heard* and that would help bring the memory back. Maybe you can picture what you were writing or saying to someone. Each time you use a sense to work with the information, you are creating a stronger pathway.

Just Do This!

Take the information in using as many senses as possible. As you are reading it, say it. Write it down! Record yourself and listen in the car. Power up your learning with multiple pathways.

Reflect and Connect:

How many senses did you usually use to study? How will this information change your behavior?

WIRE WHAT YOU'VE FIRED

1st Repetition

Pathway: _____

Description: _____

_____

_____

2nd Repetition

Pathway: _____

Description: _____

_____

_____

3rd Repetition

Pathway: _____

Description: _____

_____

_____

4th Repetition

Pathway: _____

Description: _____

_____

_____

5th Repetition

Pathway: _____

Description: _____

_____

_____

The Research:

The famous scientist John Medina says that vision trumps everything! He believes that it is the best tool of all for learning!

Half of your brain's resources are used by vision. Scientists know that vision is a very powerful tool for remembering. In fact, they call this the *pictorial superiority effect*, meaning that pictures are superior to words for remembering. Compared to reading words in a book, you can remember over six times more if you include a picture. Even pictures you imagine and don't see with your eyes are seen with visual cortex in the brain and are just as powerful.

> Instead of writing a thousand words, draw a picture!

So What?

If you play cards, you know that a trump card is the highest card in the game, no matter what. It's the best card in your hand. Well, you have a trump card in your brain, and that is vision. You learn better and remember better with pictures, including illustrations, diagrams, charts, and maps. People throughout history have known this important fact and say "a picture is worth a thousand words." So instead of writing a thousand words, or fifty words, draw a picture.

It is also important to *visualize* as you read. Try to picture what you are reading in your mind—create a mental image. If you are reading about someone doing something, picture the person doing it.

Drawing works with ideas and vocabulary words. It takes a great deal of effort to think of how to represent something with a drawing and to create the drawing, but after your brain does all that work, it is not likely to forget it.

Research for yourself which is easier to understand and remember—a picture or words? Here is a definition of *trestle* from Wikipedia:

> A **trestle** is a rigid frame used as a support, especially referring to a bridge composed of a number of short spans supported by such frames.

I mean, can you even picture this, much less recall it? But if you go to Google Image and look up *trestle,* you will see pictures similar to the ones on the right.

If you look at 3 pictures, you will learn the meaning the way the brain prefers to learn, by seeing patterns. What do the three pictures have in common? Now you know what a trestle is. If you look at the pictures first, and then read the definition, the definition then makes sense. Draw it yourself and write the definition in your own words for powerful learning.

Just Do This!

Use Google Image to look up vocabulary words. Use YouTube to watch videos of what you are studying. Take the time to sketch in the left hand column of your Smart Notes page. Try these and see the power of the *pictorial superiority effect*!

Reflect and Connect:

Do you usually look at the illustrations, pictures, charts or graphs in your textbooks? How can you use pictures to boost your memory?

The Research:

The brain naturally learns by seeing patterns and making sense of them. This contributes to how we learn language as a child without thinking about it. In fact, seeing patterns is so important to survival that when your brain sees patterns or figures something out, the brain rewards the behavior by releasing chemicals that make you feel good.

Make your thinking visual!

One way of seeing patterns is to make sense of things through categories. Instead of an alphabetical grocery list of food items, you use a list of food by category—fruits, vegetables, dairy, meat, and so forth. Then you are more likely to remember the items. The frontal lobe helps you take details and put them into broad meaningful categories, but all lobes of the brain work together. In this way, instead of isolated facts that are hard to remember, you have connected facts, a neural network, and activating part of it can make it easier to activate all of it and remember the facts.

So What?

When things make more sense and are placed into a bigger picture, they are easier to remember. Think about shopping for groceries if the foods were in random order rather than aisles with all the cereals, all the pet food, and all the vegetables. You have heard the phrase "garbage in, garbage out". This means that if you don't store information in a sensible way, you will not get sensible information back out. Information needs to be organized for better recall.

The information that you need to learn usually has a pattern in it. The pattern might be a cause and an effect such as how sun can cause sunburn, or it could be categories such as types of rocks. Use the pattern to help you remember the information. That way you are storing the information in your brain in a brain-friendly way.

Diagrams, lists, charts, and maps use the pattern of organization to present information in a visual way. This not only makes it easier to understand, it makes it easier to remember. If you write words in a list and try to recall them, you can visualize the list and perhaps remember where they were on the list. Charts and tables simplify information to make it easier to learn. Most textbooks have diagrams to make your learning easier, but students who do not know about the importance of visuals might not pay attention to them. Now you know better.

In addition to paying attention to the charts, lists, tables, diagrams, and maps it is even better if you create your own. By doing it yourself you will understand and remember it even better. Having a few handy mental "tools" in your "toolbox" can help you take advantage of this. Use some of the following diagrams when you take notes to make the pattern of organization more visual and to help you figure out what you are reading. Once you get used to using these, you will find it easier to modify these or to create new ones for yourself. Here are a few to get you started:

Compare and Contrast

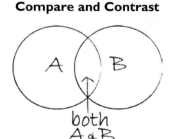

Categories

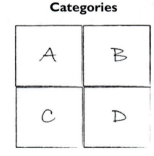

Main Idea and Details

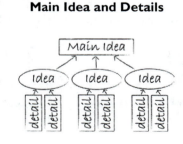

Table

	Columns ↓	Columns ↓
Rows →		
Rows →		
Rows →		
Rows →		

Mind maps are a way of getting your thoughts down in a visual way in a way similar to the way the brain works—making connections between ideas. To make a mind map, put the topic in the center and then create branches for your main ideas. Put additional ideas off the branch. This is a very important tool to help you think and brainstorm, as well as to make your notes visual. Here are a couple of ideas to get you started, but it is easy to just create your own.

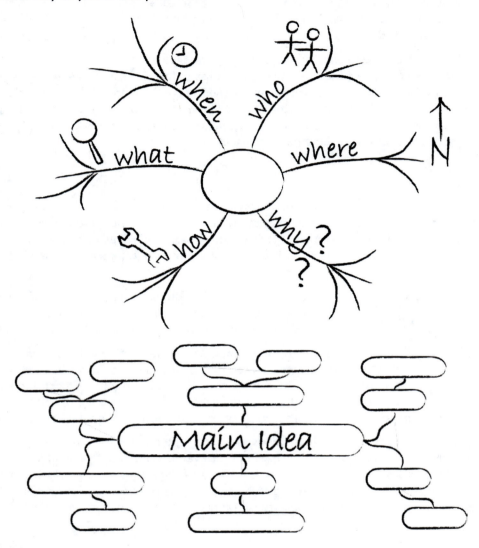

Just Do This!

Organize your notes before studying them. Study the diagrams and charts in your textbooks. Make sure you understand them. Draw your own charts, diagrams, and maps. Make your thinking visual!

Reflect and Connect:

Look back to a time when something was disorganized and it caused you a problem retrieving something? How does this relate to retrieving information? What can you do differently?

The Research:

Listening is a different brain pathway than seeing. Using both pathways together can make for a stronger experience. To the brain, there is a difference between *hearing* and *listening*. You can hear something without noticing the content of what was said. *Listening* activates the attention pathway as well, something very important to learning. In a study of monkeys, researchers found that listening to something only changed the monkeys' brains when they were *paying attention* to what they heard. If they heard it and paid attention to something else, it didn't change their brains.

> There is a difference between hearing and listening!

So What?

Be sure to take advantage of your auditory (hearing) pathway in the brain. Stay on top of your brain to make sure you are paying attention and listening carefully. Two strategies can help:

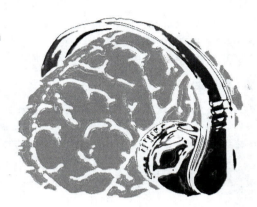

Look at the teacher as you listen. Sometimes you can remember information better later by picturing the teacher as he or she said the information—where were they standing and what did they look like?

Taking notes is a good way to help you listen better and to preserve what you hear so that you can review the material later. Taking notes also involves several senses, creating a stronger neural network, and making it easier to remember. However, you need to take notes in a smart way.

Just Do This!

Some students try to write everything down (and not everything is important, you know) and they are so busy writing that they are not really paying attention to what is said or what they are writing. Listen and think about whether something could be important and then write it down quickly. Have a system for taking notes so that you don't have to think about *how* to take notes, just about *what* to write down. You don't want too many notes on a page or you lose the visual effect. As you learned, you want to be able to *picture* your notes.

At the end of this chapter is a Smart Notes page. Make copies of this page, purchase tablets like this at the office supply store, or draw the lines on your paper and use this smart system.

Reflect and Connect:

Are you a good listener in class? How has your listening ability affected your grades?

Research

Do you ever "know it but can't say it"? Scientists understand why. It is because speaking (and writing) are different pathways in the brain from seeing (reading) and listening. Speaking and writing are "output" pathways, while reading and listening are "input" pathways. Putting information "in" is easier than getting it out—remembering it for a test or speaking an answer or another language. These pathways must be fired and wired as well. That means they must be used frequently.

> Putting information "in" is easier than getting it out.

Memory is not stored in the brain like a computer file, where it is the same every time you open it. It is stored more like a jigsaw puzzle with pieces that must be reassembled when you remember the memory. Sometimes when you try to remember—reassemble the memory—pieces are missing or you get some of the wrong pieces. This is why memory is unreliable.

Canadian researcher Colin MacLeod investigates the "production effect" which he calls a simple but powerful way to improve memory. It simply means that producing a word out loud has a better effect on memory than silently reading the word.

So What?

When is the first time you often have to get information "out" (speak it, remember it, write it)? On the test! Too late! Learners must practice *reassembling* information through speaking or writing in order to make the "output" pathway strong enough to fire again later when you need to remember something.

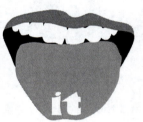

Speaking aloud is important. Reading information over and over is not enough. On the test you will need to get the information *out*. Study with a partner to get practice saying the material. Say vocabulary words aloud. Even better, say and write them at the same time. Talk yourself through math problems and the process of doing the problem will be easier to remember.

Write as much as possible. Practice explaining what you learned in your own words on paper just as you would have to do on an essay test. Take notes in class, but also take notes on your thoughts, questions, concerns, and ideas by keeping a journal. You can either make a section in your course notebook or you can buy a five section spiral notebook as a journal for all your classes. Write all kinds of thoughts and feelings you may have, as well as ideas for what might be on the test or how you think you are doing. Most importantly, write about what strategies you are trying and how they are working. A few days before the test, read through your thoughts to guide your final test preparation. Eventually you will see a pattern in how you learn and think and find ways to get even smarter.

Just Do This!

Speak and write as part of your learning and studying process.

Reflect and Connect:

When have you used speaking and writing to study? How did it work for you?

1. Test your ability to recall and use images. Think back to Week 1 and draw two neurons connecting to each other. Label the neuron, axon, dendrite, and synapse.

2. Using a current assigned reading, make a mind map of the important facts. Do this on another sheet of paper. If you are not clear on how to do a mind map, go to Google Image and type in mind map to see examples or go to http://www.wikihow.com/Make-a-Mind-Map and see the process in 11 easy steps.

3. Pick one of the sample diagrams and fill it in using information from a current assignment. Draw it on another sheet of paper.

4. Select one of the subheadings in an assigned reading. Put the term in Google Image and see if you get a timeline, chart, illustration, or diagram. If so, select two that help you understand that topic and print them if you can. If you find helpful information, you would want to continue doing this with other subheadings in that chapter.

5. Using the Smart Notes page at the end of this chapter, take notes on an assigned reading. Use all the features available to you on the form. Be sure to include drawings and questions.

6. With another student in your class, take turns teaching each other the material. Break the material down by sections and spend 3–4 minutes per turn, taking as many turns as you have time.

7. Working with one or two other students in your class, compare notes. Rewrite your notes as you compare, adding anything you missed that someone else captured. Remember that you and others may write down unimportant or incorrect information, so think critically and discuss what should go into the final notes before you write it down.

8. Experiment with talking aloud while studying. See if reading aloud, saying some of the vocabulary and important ideas aloud, or thinking aloud about the material makes a difference. Research says it will help, but you won't know until you try!

SMART NOTES

TOPIC

DATE

Drawings, Study Questions...

✓ Make drawings and sketches here later as you go through your notes or if you get time during note-taking
✓ If the teacher says "I forgot to mention" and backs up, you can write it next to the relevant material and draw an arrow
✓ As you study your notes, you can pull out important words or facts and write them here
✓ Turn the notes into questions and use them to study

Take Notes Here

✓ Spread them out so you can picture them later
✓ Only write down what might be on the test or is important to know: don't try to write everything
✓ Keep them brief
✓ Print—easier to read and recall than cursive
✓ Keep another color of ink handy to make something stand out
✓ Abbreviate – create your own symbols
   T = Test – Teacher says will be on test
   M = Memorize
   ? = Not sure – look this up
   Sp? = might not be spelled right

Write anything special here: something to be sure to do when you study; reminder of something you know will be on the test

Follow Up: to do, find out, or ask

1. How would you describe your emotions most of the time when taking a test?
   a. Calm and confident
   b. Don't think about it; doesn't affect me
   c. A little nervous or worried
   d. Very nervous: can't think, hands get sweaty, heart races

2. How does your answer above affect your performance on the test?

   _____

3. What subjects make you nervous or scared more than others? How did that affect your grade in that class? What do you do about it? Describe in several sentences:

   _____
   _____
   _____

4. Have you ever experienced a very stressful time in your life? Describe how that affected your school work.

   _____
   _____
   _____

5. How often do you play video games or online games?
   a. More than once a day
   b. About once a day
   c. About three or four times a week
   d. Maybe once a week
   e. Hardly ever

6. If you answered a, b, or c, what is it about the games that keeps you going back? What do you like about playing these games?

   _____

7. When you make mistakes in school or get answers wrong, how do you react and what do you do? Describe in 3 or 4 sentences.

   _____
   _____
   _____

8. Describe the effort and hard work that you *usually* put into studying and why.

   _____

9. Describe what part of the learning process that you actually enjoy.

   _____

The Research

School can create many situations that would make anyone nervous. Scientists study this (math, reading, or test anxiety) and the bad news is that being very nervous or having strong anxiety makes for worse performance! When your palms sweat, and your heart races, and you feel like you can't think well, you are in what scientists call "fight or flight" mode. Your body sends less fuel to your brain so that it can send the blood to your muscles. This is because you don't want to outthink the tiger, you need to outrun or fight the tiger. But we aren't scared of tigers now—we are taking tests. However, we still get this *fight or flight* reaction and this is why students do worse when they are nervous. The brain has less brain power for attention and for thinking.

> You can prevent the "fight or flight" reaction.

The good news is that scientists also know that the brain has a feed-forward and a feed-backward mechanism. Sure, sometimes the brain takes over the body and puts us in *fight or flight* mode, but our mind can take over our brain and tell it what to do—feed-backward. We can send specific messages to the brain to tell it *not* to go into that anxiety mode, but to calm down and keep the power in the brain's thinking areas.

So What?

When you get too anxious, the resources that you need to think well in class are being diverted and sent to your body instead. This means you have less brain power! It especially diminishes the power of the frontal lobes that are super important in doing well in school. The more you get nervous about how you will do, the worse you will probably do! This is what we call a vicious cycle. You do worse, and then you get more nervous. You have to break the cycle. Many people have learned how to control this and so can you.

When you are nervous, your breathing becomes fast and shallow. When you are calm and relaxed, as when you are falling asleep, your breathing becomes deep and slow. The brain knows this. You can shut off the fight or flight mechanism by changing your breathing and sending a message to the brain that all is well by taking a few, slow, deep breaths.

Just Do This!

Take control and take several slow, deep breaths before you walk into that classroom or before you take a test.

Reflect and Connect:

How have you handled test anxiety in the past and what could you do differently?

The Research:

Scientists have studied the bad effects of very high stress for many years. They have seen how high stress over a long period of time can damage health and even shrink some areas of the brain. We are not talking about being nervous in school, but about the high stress that can come from many things that numerous students experience: poverty, divorce, abuse, violence, immigration, war, natural disaster, or life-threatening situations.

Take charge and do something about high stress!

So What?

If you have experienced any of these, or something similar, you might have a level of stress that must be taken care of. Sometimes this stress shows as depression and some people turn to drugs or alcohol as well. Obviously this kind of stress is very harmful to learning. If you have this kind of high stress, be sure to let your doctor know and see what treatment is recommended. In addition, scientists have found several *interventions* that reduce the effects of this kind of stress.

- Exercise: Even a 15-minute walk has been shown to reduce depression.

- Yoga: Yoga has been shown to reduce stress and depression.

- Meditation: Many, many studies are showing the value of meditation to reduce stress, anxiety, depression, and attention problems.

- Moving meditation: Tai Chi, Chi Gong, martial arts, and meditative drumming are helpful with depression and stress.

- Gratitude: Listing three new things every day that you are grateful for has been shown to reduce stress and increase happiness.

Just Do This!

If you are having serious symptoms of depression or stress, you must take charge and do something about it. Tell your doctor and pick one of the above and begin taking control. You may also want to check out these sites:

American Psychiatric Association. 1400 K Street NW, Washington D.C. 20005. http://www.psych.org.

Anxiety Disorders Association of America, Inc. 11900 Parklawn Drive, Suite 100, Rockville, MD 20852. (301) 231-9350. http://www.adaa.org.

Childhelp USA, 15757 North 78 Street, Scottsdale, AZ 85260. 1-800-422-4453.

International Critical Incident Stress Foundation, Inc. 10176 Baltimore National Pike, Unit 201, Ellicott City, MD 21042. (410) 750-9600. Emergency: (410) 313-2473. http://www.icisf.org.

International Society for Traumatic Stress Studies. 60 Revere Drive, Suite 500, Northbrook, IL 60062. (847) 480-9028. http://www.istss.org.

National Center for PTSD. 1116D V.A. Medical Center, 215 N. Main Street, White River Junction, VT 05009-0001. (802) 296-5132. http://www.ptsd.va.gov/

National Domestic Violence Hotline 1-512-453-8117

National Helpline 1-800-662-HELP

National Institute of Mental Health. 6001 Executive Boulevard, Rm. 8184, MSC 9663, Bethesda, MD

Reflect and Connect:

What are you doing and what are you going to do to take charge of this stress?

The Research:

The brain has a *reward* system. When you do something that is important to survival, such as eating, it feels good, so that you will continue to do it. The brain *rewards* you for certain behaviors by releasing a chemical called dopamine that makes you feel happy. People love the feeling they get from dopamine, so they keep doing the behavior to get it again. One thing that triggers the chemical and rewards the brain is a sense of *progress*.

Are you going in an upward direction over time?

So What?

This is why people love video and online games—they are *rewarding* to the brain. What makes them rewarding? One important factor is that they give you a sense of *progress*. You are always aware of your score and how far you are getting. Also, as time goes on, you can see your progress in getting better at the game itself, as you go on to more difficult challenges or get higher scores. When the progress is rewarding, you work even harder, and you make even more progress. That is a cycle that works for you!

But what do we normally do in real life? We make lists or think of all the things we have to do and the list is never-ending so we always feel behind. We think of our failures and our mistakes and always feel we are never doing well enough. Not only does this work against the brain, it works against success, because happiness leads to more success.

Let's think of our bodybuilder Max M. Ize. When Max joined the gym he was given the little pink or blue weights of a pound or two. Slowly, he moved up to the bigger gray weights. Every time the trainer moved him to a bigger weight, Max felt a sense of pride and left the gym feeling great. Imagine how Max would feel if the trainer never moved him up, or didn't tell him that the new weights were actually heavier. Max wouldn't feel like he was getting anywhere and would probably give up and quit. What if Max kept looking at the other weight lifters who had the huge weights? He could keep comparing himself to them and keep saying "I am not as good as them and probably never will be" and could give up on himself. But what if the trainer showed him how many weights he had worked through so far and how he was getting stronger and stronger. Max would feel great, even though he was not yet caught up with the others.

Max would have good days and bad days. If he went on vacation and didn't practice, he could come back to the gym and find that he couldn't lift what he was lifting before and had to be moved back a size or two. Should Max give up and say he would never succeed? No, because the trainer knows that we do not progress in a straight line. It is natural and normal to have progress that goes up and down. The important question is "Are you going in an upward direction over time?"

Write down every day one way in which you are making progress or doing better (you cleaned your closet, you fixed something, you got a new app, you turned in your homework on time, you studied harder than usual—anything). You will soon see that you are moving forward toward your goals!

If you show your brain that you are making progress, you are going to reward the brain and body for the progress. This makes it more likely that you will continue to make progress. In this case, we will see progress in your grades going up.

Let's figure out how you can see progress, because it isn't what the other person is doing, but whether your own brain is getting better. Here are some graphs that show progress. Notice that they do not go up in a straight line. Sometimes we have normal setbacks, but we keep working and the line goes back up.

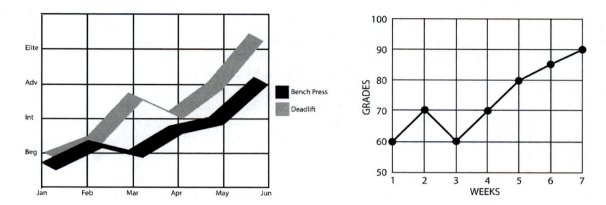

Practice putting some numbers on the graph below. Plot the following grades for the last six tests that Marie took. Let's do the first one: 70. Starting at the left above the number one (for test one) go up to the number 70. Place a large dot there. On test two Marie dropped down to 65. Above the number 2, go up to halfway between 60 and 70 and place a dot on the line. Now do the next four tests: 80, 75, 85, and 90. Now draw a line connecting the dots. Did the line end higher than when it started? That's progress!

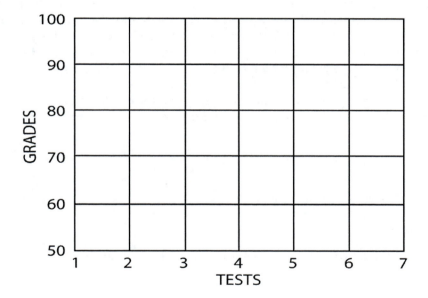

Just Do This!

Track your progress on the chart at the end of the chapter. Once you see that this rewards your brain and motivates you, keep doing it!

Reflect and Connect:

Do you only focus on your mistakes and failures instead of your progress? Is this what you do when you play video or online games? What could you do differently?

The Research:

Scientists discovered something called the "learning paradox." You may know that a paradox is something that seems like it wouldn't be true but it is, such as the paradox that standing is actually more tiring than walking. The learning paradox is that the more you struggle and the more you fail when you are in the process of learning, the more you are actually learning! Yes, struggle and failure are good— they are a natural and important part of the learning process. Scientists also have a term invented by a researcher in Singapore named Manu Kapur, called "productive failure." This means that when learners are not immediately taught how to do something but allowed to struggle with it themselves for a while, they learn better. He studied math students and those who worked with other students to figure it out without being told and who made lots of mistakes (productive failure) did much better than the students who were just told how to do it from the beginning. Struggles in learning help students understand material more deeply.

When the brain learns, it not only grows new dendrites and expands, it also cuts back or "prunes" some dendrites and connections; it becomes more efficient. Making lots of mistakes helps the brain reorganize itself into more efficient pathways. Neuroscientist Michael Kilgard suggests that once the brain figures out what works and what doesn't, it can prune away connections that are no longer needed to make the brain more efficient.

Struggle and failure are a natural part of the learning process!

So What?

We should never feel ashamed or bad about our mistakes, but look at them as getting closer to understanding. Even Einstein had a long list of mistakes! Long! Michael Jordan, the famous basketball player, says that he has missed more than 9,000 shots in his career! He has lost almost 300 games and been given the ball to make the winning shot and missed it 26 times! Does he consider himself a failure? No. He says that because he has failed over and over again, he is a success. For example, when you learn a physical skill, such as skating for example, you may lean in different directions and try many postures at first, most of which may result in falling down. These mistakes help the body find the right balance and movement to make turns or go faster until eventually you form a fluent pathway. Then your muscle memory takes over: your muscles learned and automatically know how to move without your thinking because the cells that fired together, wired together.

Just Do This!

Make mistakes, fail, work hard, never give up, and be a success!

Reflect and Connect:

How have mistakes in the past helped you when you were learning? Has your attitude toward mistakes changed?

The Research

Scientists have discovered that *effort* is part of the reward pathway. Things you work harder to achieve give you a bigger reward—you get that feel good chemical of dopamine. If humans didn't work hard, they would not survive long—therefore, effort is part of the brain's survival/reward pathway. The brain rewards *effort and hard work*.

> Things you work harder to achieve give you a bigger reward!

Another activity that releases feel-good chemicals in the brain is when our brain figures something out. If we couldn't figure things out, we wouldn't survive either, so that activates the survival/reward pathway.

So What?

When you work puzzles, do you choose the easy 10-piece one or the 500-piece one? Why? When you win every game on a level in a video or online game, do you stay at that level so that you keep winning every game, or do you move on to a harder level? If a weight lifter lifted only the little 1- and 2-pound pink and blue weights to be sure to succeed, how would he feel? Why would he go back? What does he really do? Why do people move to a harder level when they have to put out more mental effort? Because it feels good, that's why. We love a challenge.

Humans love challenges. This is why we strive to become better at sports or crafting or cooking or anything. We feel so good after a job well done. If you want to feel better about school and learning, then work harder! We feel better when we work harder. One reason some students don't want to work too hard (and deprive themselves of this good feeling) is because of fear. They are afraid they will fail and if they put a good deal of effort into something and they fail they feel worse than if they didn't try. Don't choose what might make you feel less worse! Choose what will make you feel better. Effort. If you don't succeed, you have the good feeling that you tried hard and gave it your best and now you know that your mistakes are also helpful!

Another way students go wrong is wanting the teacher to tell them everything that will be on the test so they can just memorize it. Memorizing doesn't feel good. Figuring things out and learning feel good.

Just Do This!

Work harder! Think! Ask questions! Figure things out for yourself! Lift those "heavy weights"!

Reflect and Connect:

Do you avoid feeling worse or do you want to feel better? What is stopping you from putting forth more effort?

TRACK YOUR PROGRESS

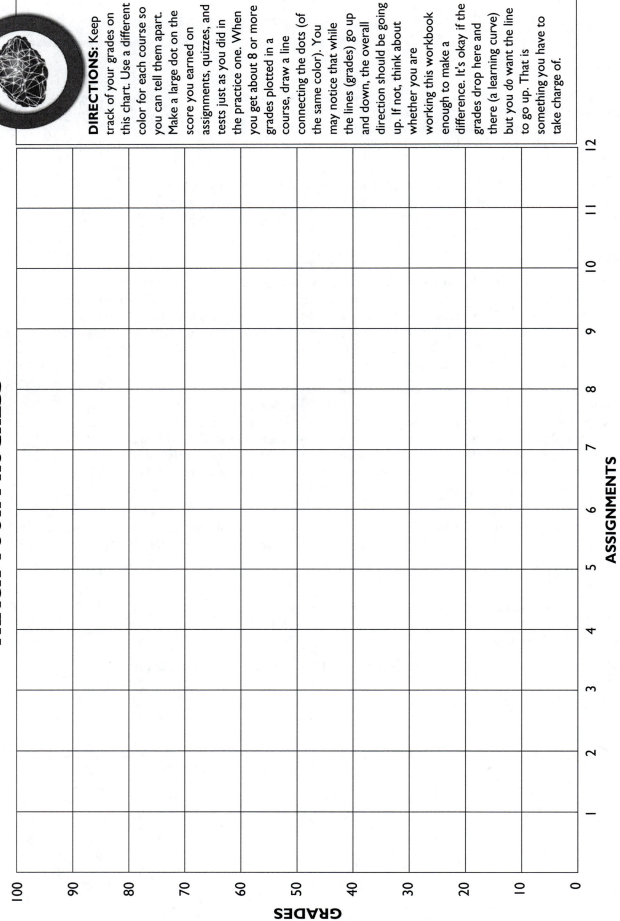

WIRE IT

DIRECTIONS: Keep track of your grades on this chart. Use a different color for each course so you can tell them apart. Make a large dot on the score you earned on assignments, quizzes, and tests just as you did in the practice one. When you get about **8** or more grades plotted in a course, draw a line connecting the dots (of the same color). You may notice that while the lines (grades) go up and down, the overall direction should be going up. If not, think about whether you are working this workbook enough to make a difference. It's okay if the grades drop here and there (a learning curve) but you *do* want the line to go up. That is something you have to take charge of.

GRADES

100 90 80 70 60 50 40 30 20 10 0

ASSIGNMENTS

1 2 3 4 5 6 7 8 9 10 11 12

COLOR KEY:

FIRE IT

Check Your Frontal Lobes

Write the number in the blank that best describes how you **usually** behave. Answer **honestly** so you can find out how to improve your brain.

5) always   4) most of the time   3) maybe   2) not very often   1) never

_____ 1. I plan ahead when I will actually do an assignment.

_____ 2. I use a planner to keep track of all assignments.

_____ 3. I begin an assignment early; I do not wait until the night before it is due.

_____ 4. When I read, I think about whether I understand something.

_____ 5. If I do not understand what I am reading, I back up and read it over.

_____ 6. I allow enough time for all assignments to get done.

_____ 7. I keep an organized notebook.

_____ 8. I plan how to do a long assignment before I start.

_____ 9. I break long assignments down into smaller steps and work on them over a period of days.

_____ 10. I meet deadlines for turning in material.

_____ 11. When I get a graded paper back, I think about why I got answers wrong and then about what to change to do better.

_____ 12. If I don't like a grade, I think about how I can do something differently.

_____ 13. I control my emotions in class.

_____ 14. I don't interrupt others or speak out of turn in class.

_____ 15. I don't listen to music or have social media active when I study.

_____ 16. I can stay focused on what I am doing and not get distracted.

_____ 17. I have my supplies and materials with me when I need them.

_____ 18. I set goals for myself.

How are you doing now? Add your points and check your score.

72+   You are in charge of your mind and your behavior! You are doing well and on the road to success! The more of these skills you add, and the better you get at them, the better your life will be!

71–37   You will benefit greatly from doing the activities in this chapter. Do all of them, add new habits, and experience better learning! You can learn to take better control of your brain and your performance.

0–36   You **can** change your brain and raise this score. Devote yourself wholeheartedly to this chapter. Keep doing all the new strategies that you learn, adding to your skills and habits. Watch other students and learn from their skills. You can create a better brain and better outcomes in your life if you work hard on these skills. Do this for yourself and your future. You will make progress and see results!

The Research

Picture yourself back in kindergarten while you read about this research study. Scientists followed children in kindergarten until they were adults and made an amazing discovery! They found one behavior in children that predicted how well they would do in school the rest of their life and even their income, drug use, and criminal behavior! All it took was teacher observation to rate the children and then they compared all of the previous outcomes with one behavior—the ability to control themselves. Did they raise their hand before speaking, stay in line, wait their turn, and control their behavior? This ability predicted the quality of the rest of their life!

> "Good frontal lobes, good life."

Self-regulation and self-monitoring (controlling yourself and watching and thinking about what you do) are important skills for school success. In a study of 320 college students, Dr. Carol Van Zile-Tamsen found that those with the lowest grade average had the worst self-regulation. However, if those with poor grades became motivated to learn the course material, they became better self-regulators. They improved their frontal lobes. In another study, Dr. Barry Zimmerman found that when students set goals and monitored their behavior, they raised their performance by 30%. That's a lot!

The frontal lobes are in the front of your brain, behind your forehead. They are very important to a successful life because they regulate much of the brain's activity and help you make better choices. They are involved in "executive functions," the kind of thing an important executive would do, such as:

- Planning
- Organizing information
- Budgeting time, money, or resources
- Meeting deadlines
- Using good judgment

- Controlling attention
- Controlling emotion
- Regulating behavior
- Avoiding distractions
- Setting goals and achieving them

Neuroscientist Jay Giedd studies teenagers' brain development and says adolescence is a "use it or lose it" time and suggests practice as important to keeping the brain skills that you want. He says you are hard-wiring your brain during this time so think about the brain that you want.

So What?

In our brain research lab we used to say "Good frontal lobes, good life, bad frontal lobes, bad life!" Your frontal lobes help you control what is in your brain. This is the skill you use to take charge of your brain.

If you feel that you would have scored poorly on self-control in kindergarten, it is not too late. Frontal lobes continue to develop until around age 25. In fact, teenagers go through a major overhaul of their brain as it gets rewired for adulthood. This is a very important time for working at developing your brain. Even after age 25 we can improve, but it takes a little more effort and persistence.

If someone cuts you off in traffic or makes you angry in some way, your frontal lobes can help you think through your response. They can put the brakes on the emotion and you can realize that punching someone may not be the best response. Controlling your emotions (anxiety, anger, frustration, discouragement) are important to school and life success and demonstrate that you have a good brain. Also,

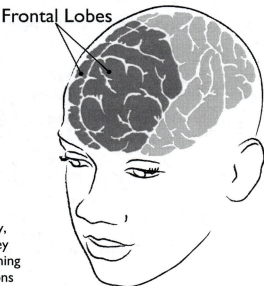

Frontal Lobes

the frontal lobes help you regulate your attention so that you can stay focused and finish the task you started. Good frontal lobes are what enable people to keep working without giving up or getting off track. Good frontal lobes help you with completing assignments and with writing papers.

Maybe the most important thing you could do for your own school success and success in life would be to improve your frontal lobes—your executive functions in the list above. How? You improve frontal lobes the same way you develop any part of your brain and the way you develop skills: by doing it, by using them. Your frontal lobes develop by using them—by giving more thought to your behavior and your thinking processes and by doing the kinds of things in the list. You can make an effort to "put your frontal lobes in gear" and plan, organize, and make good decisions. The more you work at the skills listed in the bullet points above, the better you will get at them. Of course, upgrading your brain isn't easy, so this will take effort and persistence but the gains are huge!

Planning is an important function of the frontal lobes and a key to success in school and life. Plan out your study schedule and how much time you will need for each subject. Here is a hint: Getting started is the hardest part of an assignment, especially a long term assignment. When faced with a difficult or long assignment, get a timer (most phones have one). Set the timer for 20 minutes and tell yourself you just have to work for that long. You can stand anything for 20 minutes, right? By the time the timer goes off you may be well into the project and not even want to stop. If not, then just work on this 20 minutes at a time or longer if possible until the project is done.

Just Do This!

Work hard on this chapter. *Think* about your brain processes and your behaviors. Start by beginning the Firing Activity: How Good Are You at Planning Your Time?

Reflect and Connect:

How good do you think your frontal lobes are based on previous decisions and performance in your life? Are you ready to work on them?

Checking in with my Brain	
THE MOST USEFUL THING I LEARNED IN THIS UNIT WAS:	
THE NEW STRATEGIES THAT I TRIED WERE:	
Strategy	How did it work for me?
WHAT WILL I KEEP DOING?	
WHAT PREVIOUS HABITS WILL I CHANGE?	
WHAT PROGRESS AM I MAKING?	

The Research:

Metacognition is a term that means *thinking about your thinking*. (*Meta* means beyond or self and *cognition* means thinking). It is linked to insight (seeing in) and *reflection* (thinking back about something). Have you ever said to yourself, "What was I thinking?" Good! That's using metacognition, an important brain skill.

Brain researcher Dr. Steve Fleming says that reflecting on your thoughts and behaviors is critical for making good decisions. He says people who don't aren't going to have a very smooth life. He found that people who were more accurate at evaluating how well they did had more gray matter (brain cells) in their frontal lobes than those who weren't as accurate.

> Do you keep doing the same thing and expect a different result?

So What?

By thinking about your thinking and your behavior, you can create a better brain! Who doesn't need that? How aware are you of yourself? Do you think you did well on a test and find that you did not or think that you did not but found that you did do well? Neither of these outcomes shows accurate self-awareness. By practicing predicting your grades, you should get better at it over time and better at metacognition.

One important skill of metacognition is to plan out a *strategy*. In school, this would mean thinking about all the learning strategies you know and deciding which ones would be best for a particular learning situation. Some examples of strategies are

- taking notes
- making it visual
- using flash cards
- tape-recording and listening
- using several senses

These are just a few and you will learn more as you work through this book. Then when you have done the assignment and received a grade, think about how well that strategy actually worked and make a plan for future similar situations to either continue the strategy or get a new one. You know what they say: *Insanity is doing the same thing and expecting different results.*

Other ways to develop metacognition to upgrade your brain are: connect what you are learning to what you already know, think out loud, and set goals. It is important to keep a journal of your thoughts, behaviors, decisions, and outcomes and read it over to see how you are doing. Use the handout called Metacognition at the end of this chapter with every assignment until this behavior comes naturally to you.

Just Do This!

Upgrade your brain by thinking about your thought processes and your behaviors.

Reflect and Connect:

How often do you pause and evaluate your behavior? How well do you know yourself?

The Research

Do you ever feel "brain dead" or more tired from thinking hard than if you had worked physically hard? Scientists call that *cognitive load*. Cognitive means thinking and so this means the heavy thinking load that your brain is carrying. It is not true that we only use 10% of our brains. In fact, we are often on cognitive overload where we have too much on our minds or are working our brains very hard.

Scientists have seen through brain scans that when someone is learning something new, their brain works harder than when they have practiced it. It is like when you first learned to drive a car, you had heavy cognitive load ("don't talk to me, turn the radio down) and you had to concentrate very hard. Now, when you drive, since you are so practiced, you don't have to think about it so much and you carry on conversations (or risk your life texting). Doing executive function tasks, working in a second language, distractions, and being stressed can all increase the cognitive load.

Even though the brain is only about 3% of your body weight, it uses 20% of your body's fuel intake! Fifteen minutes of heavy thinking can be to the brain like 15 minutes in a gym is to the body.

> *Are you on cognitive overload?*

So What?

Max, the bodybuilder, knows that he can't lift weights continuously over a period of time. Instead, he does enough repetitions until he feels the muscles get tired, rests a bit, and then begins again. This is how you should think of your brain.

When you are putting forth a great deal of mental effort, such as reading difficult material, memorizing, working problems, or studying for a test, take a mental break about every 20 minutes. No, not a *break* break. A mental break. Doodle or sketch and let your brain rest a little while it is making connections and *consolidating* (strengthening learning. Get up and stretch, take the dog out briefly, throw in a load of laundry, lay out your clothes for the next day, or get some water). The break should only be 1-3 minutes, unless you have been studying for many segments. Then it would be helpful to take the best kind of brain break—a nap (more on that later). Break long assignments into segments.

You can't work physically hard when you are tired and you can't learn well when you are mentally tired. Cramming just exhausts the brain! Do you study right before the test? Would you wear yourself out working out in the gym right before a strength competition? No! The day of the test, carry a light mental load.

Just Do This!

Be metacognitive—pay attention to whether your brain is getting tired. Plan your study time so you can take frequent breaks.

Reflect and Connect:

Which assignments give you heavy cognitive load?

The Research:

Scientists have a term for multitasking: *divided attention*. Think about what that term is telling you. Scientists have looked into the brains of people who multitask and found that they are *not* doing two or more things at once. No, they are *dividing* their attention. Worse, they are alternating attention between the tasks and when they do, they lose a great deal of time and thought.

Because students multitask so much now—studying with the TV, Internet, email, messaging, social media, and headphones—students believe that they are good at it. So scientists studied them, thinking maybe the new generation has better attention, more working memory capacity, or more cognitive flexibility. They found out that the students were *not* better at any of those things and, worse, multitasking made them perform worse on the tasks. They only *thought* they were doing well. (Metacognition would have helped here!)

Scientists also studied many multitaskers and found out that those who thought they were the *best* at multitasking were actually the *worst*. Those who thought they couldn't multitask well were the best performers because they realized that multitasking drains the brain—it *increases cognitive load*. The researchers believe that those who think they do well with multitasking are actually seeking *distraction from* their work.

Scientists have not found anything good about this practice. All evidence points to the benefits of avoiding distraction. All distractions, including music and instant messages, increase the cognitive load, making the brain get tired faster and work less well. Although the brain can learn an unlimited amount of information, it can only *process* a certain amount at a time, similar to the RAM on a computer. Every single distraction (multitasking) uses part of the brain's resources, leaving less for the actual learning task.

Multitasking drains the brain.

So What?

This means that the more distractions such as email, social media, Internet, music, TV and so forth you allow into your study environment, the less brain power you have for learning. Don't say that these things are not distractions, because they are. They use brain resources. Listen to the science and make the smart decision.

Just Do This!

Do not multitask when studying. Experience your brain on multitasking yourself with the assignment at the end called "Your Brain on Multitasking."

Reflect and Connect:

What are your most tempting distractions? How can you reduce distractions while studying?

The Research

Recall in week two when you learned that it was only when the monkeys *paid attention* to something that their brains changed. They could do the same thing without paying attention and nothing happened. It is *what* you are paying attention to that matters.

The frontal lobes play an important role in controlling attention. People who can't control their attention have a difficult time in school, as they are constantly missing information or doing poorly because their attention is distracted constantly. Good frontal lobe attention skill means that you can consciously direct and maintain focus on something over a period of time and not pay attention to other things. This is called *selective attention* and is the kind of attention necessary in school.

Scientists have studied *mindfulness meditation* (focusing attention on awareness of the moment without judging or thinking about it) and the brains of those who engage in this practice. They found that people who meditate have better attention and more gray matter in important areas—better brains. They discovered that brains could change in a few weeks with minimal practice.

> It isn't the time you spend studying, it is the attention.

So What?

What does it mean when a teacher says "pay attention"? Do you think it means take in *more* information? Actually, it means taking in less. Instead of your awareness being like a big bright security light, lighting up everything in the area, good attention is like a powerful flashlight, lighting up one specific area of importance. It is the ability to direct and hold *focus*.

Have you ever been driving somewhere thinking about something and all of a sudden you are there and don't even remember the drive? Or you read an assignment and suddenly realize you have no idea what you just read because your eyes were seeing the words but your mind was *paying attention* to something else.

Attention drives learning! When you are in class or doing an assignment, use your mind to think about what your brain is paying attention to. Try out your selective attention ability. Go to http://www.theinvisiblegorilla.com/videos.html#tryit and click on the first video. If you do not have good attention skill, then investigate mindfulness meditation. You *can* improve your brain!

Just Do This!

Keep checking in with yourself, self-monitoring, to make sure your brain is paying attention to what is necessary in order to learn and change.

Reflect and Connect:

How would you describe your attention skills? What are you going to do to get better?

How Good Are You at Planning Time?

Complete this form over the next 10 assignments. Depending upon how many assignments you get in a day, this may only take a few days. After it is completed, answer the questions at the end as honestly as possible so that you can learn how to improve your brain and learning.

	Subject	Assignment	Estimated time to complete	Actual time to complete	Grade earned on assignment	Difference in minutes + or –
1						
2						
3						
4						
5						
6						
7						
8						
9						
10						

TOTAL SCORE OF MINUTES

Add all of the + scores and then add the – scores. Subtract the – scores from the + total, for a final score. Write it in the box next to Total Score of Minutes.

Now answer the following questions:

1. Did you get a positive (you had time left over) or a negative score (you did not budget enough time)?

    _____

2. Why did this happen to you?

    _____

3. As time went on toward the bottom of the chart, did you get closer to the estimated time? _____

4. If you had a negative score and the answer to #3 is "no", then you need improvement in time management. This is a skill that can be learned. You can improve your brain in this function. What will you do differently to achieve this? How will you change your behavior to improve your brain?

    _____

TIP: If you did not do well on this, then track this information until you actually get within 15 minutes of the estimated time at least five times in a row. Then you no longer need to track it because you have learned to use this function in your brain better.

Study Reading Plan for Learning While You Read

Use your frontal lobes well when you are reading assignments. Asking questions as you read and testing yourself as you go is an amazing way to learn while you are reading assigned material. It doesn't take much longer and you get more results for time spent. Let's do what works!

You want to do two important activities when you read material. You want to *annotate* your book, which, yes, means writing in the book. I know they are expensive, but not as expensive as retaking a course. Time is money, too. When you annotate, you are using more of your senses and creating a stronger memory. You also want to reduce the information into a manageable form for studying, by taking notes on the important information. You can do both at the same time.

On the next page is the plan. Make a copy of the plan for all of your course notebooks and put it in the front. At first, refer to the help in the column at the right. Once this type of smart thinking becomes a habit, you won't need to look at the right hand column. You can just run through the steps at the left. Eventually, you won't even need this page anymore to make sure that you are learning while you read.

Checking in with my Brain	
THE MOST USEFUL THING I LEARNED IN THIS UNIT WAS:	
THE NEW STRATEGIES THAT I TRIED WERE:	
Strategy	How did it work for me?
WHAT WILL I KEEP DOING?	
WHAT PREVIOUS HABITS WILL I CHANGE?	
WHAT PROGRESS AM I MAKING?	

Study Reading Plan for Learning While You Read

BEFORE READING

1. How does this relate to what I already know?	How can I make a connection to my existing neural network? Is there something similar to this that I know? This is the most important question. Maybe write down what you already know in the box at the bottom of the Smart Notetaking Page.
2. Ask yourself why am I reading this—to understand? To memorize? To apply?	This will tell you what kind of notes to take and what to look for and how to study. Jot down the purpose at the top of your notes page.
3. Flip through the chapter looking at the headings and subheadings to give your brain some categories in which to place the new information.	Continue asking yourself what do I already know about these? What is the relationship between the headings? Turn these into questions and write them in the column on the left on your notes page.

DURING READING

4. Predict. Think about what you expect to discover.	Guess where the author is going with this. Guess what is going to happen next. Don't write these down: just think.
5. Ask *is* this important to know? If so, *why?* Is the author telling me this to help me understand something else or is this something I need to know for the test?	If you think this is something you need to know for the test, write a big T next to it. You might draw a vertical line in the margin next to the paragraph so that when you go back to take notes you can condense the section into your notes.
6. What is not clear?	Mark with a ? and make a note in the Follow Up Box at the bottom of your notes page. If this is a confusing vocabulary word, do an Internet search and clear up the confusion before continuing. Write the meaning of these words in the margin so when you review the material to take notes, you will recall the meaning. You can also write the words and their meaning in the left-hand column of the Super Notetaking Page.
7. As you read, continue to make connections with what you already know.	Make notes in the margins. For example, if you were reading about how the many parts of the brain all work together, you might write "like an orchestra". This will help you remember.
8. Watch for and mark patterns of organization.	If a paragraph or section contains a list (using words such as first, another, a third, also) number the sentences. This will help you remember and make it easier to take notes.

AFTER READING

9. Organize and reformat. How is the information organized? Are there categories, lists, definitions, examples?	Organize the information as you take notes. Number items in a list. Write EX for example.
10. Use your visual strengths to condense the information and make it easy to recall by using pictures or maps and diagrams.	Use diagrams and maps to make the information visible and to show relationships.
11. Review how this relates to what you already know.	Write down any new connections that you have made to something similar that can help you understand or recall this information.

1. Turn to the Zadina Model of Academic Memory Processes at the end of this chapter. The boxes down the left and right side refer to strategies that help people remember. Some of these you will recognize and some maybe not. For as many as you can, complete this chart:

Strategy	What it Means	Example of When I Used It (course, material)	How Well Did It Work For Me?
Rehearsal and Repetition			
Chunking			
Mnemonics			
Associations & Connection (Existing Neural Networks)			
Reformatting			
Multiple Pathways			
Attention; Emotion			
Survival & Importance; Real Life Experiences			
Context			

2. Students use many strategies when they read textbooks or study for tests. Below are some of them. Circle the ones that you use on a regular basis:

- Highlighting

- Underlining

- Rereading

- Taking notes

- Quizzing myself or doing practice tests

- Cramming a day or two before the test

- Spacing out my studying over a period of time

- Flash cards

- Quizzing a friend

- Write down material over and over

- Put it in a different form, such as a drawing, mind map, or list

- Say it out loud

- Think about how it relates to real life

- Make connections to what I already know

- Get excited or emotionally involved

- Other _____

- Other _____

News Flash! Two of these are the best two according to scientists. They get the job done! Two are more common, but don't really have much effect on learning. In this chapter you will learn the important difference.

Now underline the two that scientists say are the best for learning.

3. Do you ever lose your train of thought when reading or doing a math problem and have to start back at the beginning again? Give an example.

   _____

4. Do you have trouble remembering something long enough to write it down? Give an example.

   _____

   _____

5. Complete this expression: Practice makes _____. What does this mean? How would this apply to studying?

The Research

Remember the Hebbian Law: *cells that fire together, wire together*. To learn it is necessary to fire the neural network repeatedly until it is strong and stable. You need to achieve *long term potentiation* which means that the more a group of neurons fire together, the more likely they are to fire together again, which is *learning*. Repetition is essential for learning study material.

However, some firings are stronger than other firings. When you hardly pay attention or you don't care, the firing may be weak, and require much more repetition. But if it is funny or scary or really interesting to you and you are paying close attention, then the firing can be very strong, sometimes so strong you don't even need more repetition. Much of the strength of the firing depends upon the importance of the information to the *learner*. A researcher named Hermann Ebbinghaus said that it is not enough to learn something, you must *overlearn* it so that you can remember it over time.

So What?

Just as you have to keep working a muscle to make it strong through many repetitions, so with your neural network. Keep firing the network by thinking and doing things. This means lots of repetition. Repeat—fire it until you wire it. Now that doesn't mean just rereading it over and over. So far in this book you learned many ways to work with material. One of the important things you learned is to use as many senses as possible: see it, say it, hear it, write it, and draw it. In the last chapter you learned to think about the material more deeply, which is a powerful way to fire and wire. You learned to study-read, another way to repeat and wire. In this chapter you will learn some powerful ways to *encode* memory—to make it stick in the brain. Some of these you may know as study strategies, but others come from recent neuroscience, such as the importance of emotion and attention on memory.

Just Do This!

Fire it until you wire it. Repeat, repeat, repeat **but** in many different ways.

Reflect and Connect:

Have you built repetition into your studying?

The Research:

You can probably guess the difference between short-term memory and long-term memory. Before you can have long-term memory you must have some short-term memory, now called *working memory*. Working memory is what you hold in your active mind briefly while you work with it. You remember a phone number long enough to call it. You remember parts of a math problem long enough to work it and parts of a sentence long enough to get to the end of the sentence and understand it. Or do you? Researchers have found that much of what seems to be math difficulty or reading comprehension difficulty is actually working memory difficulty. The student can't hold the first part of the information "online" long enough to work the problem or comprehend the sentence or paragraph.

Before you can have long-term memory, you must have some working memory.

All humans have a working memory *capacity*—how much they can hold in their mind briefly. However, for even the best minds, the upper limit seems to be 4–7 items (numbers in a phone number, parts of a math problem). New research indicates that it may be even less. Some people have poor working memory capacity and this strongly affects their school performance.

So What?

You may be having trouble in school because you have trouble with working memory. Working memory can be improved through training using the same process you make any brain changes with—by doing it. In addition, new research shows that playing a musical instrument or meditating improves working memory.

But in the meantime, what can you do? Education experts have found some tricks that we can use to extend our working memory capacity. One *is rehearsal and repetition*, such as when you say the phone number over and over until you can finish writing it down. Do you use this strategy when you study? Do you say the first part of the math problem to yourself or aloud so that you can remember it as you work? Talking aloud helps. Try the same thing with reading. Pause and picture what is happening, then continue. Repeat it to yourself as you go.

Another strategy is called *chunking*. Take something long and break it into a few chunks so it fits into your working memory capacity. For example, it would be hard to remember 7277285318 but you could remember 727-728-5318. Now instead of 10 items, it is 3 items—three chunks. When doing math, write down the individual steps instead of trying to hold them in your memory. Break down the sentence or paragraph into smaller pieces. Then reread it. Remember, the purpose of working memory is to hold it in your head long enough to complete an action—not long-term for a test. That comes next.

Just Do This!

Break things down. Talk aloud.

Reflect and Connect:

Do you have trouble getting things down on paper? How do you think this affects your learning? What can you do about it?

The Research

You can't remember something just because you want to, or because you hear it or see it. For school material, information must be *actively encoded* in the brain—something must be done to convert it from working memory (what you just read or heard) to *long-term memory* (long-term storage in the brain from which you can retrieve information later).

The more ways you encode memory, the stronger the memory!

Look again at the **Zadina Model of Academic Memory Processes** at the end of this chapter. Notice what happens. First the information comes in through your senses visual (see it) or auditory (hear it). Then it goes into Working Memory (temporary storage). You see to the left and right the two strategies for holding it there longer that you just learned. Next you see a section called *Encoding Process*. To the left and right are strategies that help you encode—convert—this into long-term storage. Keep in mind that you must do *active* things to encode memory, but you can choose the type according to your preferences or the type of material. However, researchers know that the more ways you encode memory, the stronger the memory—the neural network. Researchers looked at students all over the world and found that students who used good strategies to understand and remember performed *two grade levels* better on a standardized test than those who didn't use strategies.

Rehearsal and repetition: As you learned, repetition is essential to learning. Build it into your study plan.

Mnemonics: This strategy helps you remember something by creating a shortcut saying, such as Please Excuse My Dear Aunt Sally helps you remember the order of operations in math (parenthesis, exponents, multiplication, division, addition, and subtraction) by looking at the first letter in this easy-to-remember phrase. You can create these yourself. The funnier you make them, the easier to remember.

Chunking: You learned this in the last lesson.

Associations and Connections: Association is linking one thing to something easier to remember. To remember Mr. Brown's name, you might associate it with his brown hair. Connecting new information to what you already know is an important strategy that you learned the first week of this course.

Reformatting: Put the material in an easier-to-remember format. Draw it. Make it into a list, map, chart. Break long sentences down into shorter sentences or parts of sentences with key words. Put it into categories.

Multiple Pathways: As you know, the more senses you use when you study, the better you remember.

So What?

The more of these you use, the stronger the learning and the bigger your neural network. For every assignment, look at the Zadina Model and figure out which strategies will work for that assignment. For example, learning vocabulary words might use repetition with flash cards, associations, and multiple pathways.

Just Do This!

Use the strategies! Get good at using them! They work!

Reflect and Connect:

Which of these have you used in the past? Why or why not?

The Research:

Researchers have discovered that sometimes the neurons fire stronger than other times, creating a stronger memory from the beginning. This would make learning easier, since your goal is to create a strong network. What kinds of things might make stronger firing?

Cut down your study time and make it easier to remember!

Attention: Remember the monkeys? It is not what you do as much as the attention you bring to it that changes the brain. Since learning is a brain change, you want to bring strong attention to the task.

Survival & Importance to the Learner: This is more important than repetition. How many times do you have to stick your hand in the fire to learn it is hot? We know that people learn what is important to them. How hard was it for you to learn to use a cell phone and apps?

Real-life Experiences & Meaning: Researchers divided students into two groups. One group had to write a summary every day of the lesson. Hard work! The other group just had to come up with a way that the daily material related to real life. At semester's end, the second group did much better.

The meaning of something is a very important factor in remembering. It is very heard to remember something that is meaningless, but something that makes sense or is meaningful is much easier to remember. Therefore, creating meaning out of what you read will help you encode it into memory. Think about what this information means in real-life or in the big picture.

Context: Researchers know that material out of context (surrounding information) is harder to learn. Look at the sports headlines in the paper or online. If you didn't know it was sports, those headings would make no sense.

Existing Neural Networks: The more you already know about something, the easier it is to learn. That is why some students seem smarter—they already have a neural network. Sometimes you need to back up and create a stronger network or get on the Internet and learn more.

Emotion: This is the most important one of all! If something is really exciting or scary or affects you emotionally, it fires much more strongly.

So What?

No multitasking. Get in there and one and done! Tie what you learn into something important to you—not just the grade but a later outcome. Think about growing a better brain if for no other reason. Explore it on the internet and watch videos to see how facts fit into the big picture. Force yourself to get emotionally involved with the topic. These things will cut down your study time.

Just Do This!

These enhancements cut down study time and make it easier to remember. Use them!

Reflect and Connect:

Describe a time when one of these created a really strong memory of something in school.

The Research

For over 100 years, researchers have known that there is one study strategy that is better than all the others but you may not have even tried it. That strategy is *practice testing.* Psychologist Regan Gurung found that college students who used practice tests got higher grades. A team of researchers led by Mark McDaniel found that when middle school teachers gave their students daily practice tests, the students did better on the exam.

> Space out your studying and practice test for higher grades!

We can understand the reason behind the success of this strategy when we look inside the brain. The brain has both receptive and expressive pathways. This just means that you can take information *in*, such as through listening and reading. You can also *express* information through speaking and writing. What are you doing when you are taking a test? You are not taking the information in, such as when you are reading material over and over. No, you are pulling the information out—expressing it. That expressive pathway must be fired and wired. So the brain is better prepared for the test when it has practiced what it will be required to do on the test—getting the information out rather than taking it in.

Researchers John Dunlosky and his coworkers discovered that another special strategy made a big difference in grades. They call it *distributed practice.* This means spacing out the studying over a period of time rather than doing it in large blocks of time right before the test (cramming). Researchers Landrum, Turrisi, and Brandel found that students who got A's and B's on the test actually spent **less** time studying during each study session compared to those go got D's or F's. **However,** they studied more often as the semester went along. The A students knew a secret that the researchers proved to be true: you learn more when you spread out the studying into shorter sessions over a longer period of time. They did much better than students who tried to do all their studying in long sessions prior to the test (cramming). The strategy that *works* is called *distributed practice.*

Researcher Daniel Willingham and colleagues found out the two study strategies that students use the *most,* were actually the *worst!* Can you guess? Highlighting and underlining were the two least helpful strategies for getting better results. This may be because it is done rather mindlessly. Remember that attention is key to changing the brain.

So What?

It is okay if you want to underline or highlight to help yourself focus, but do not think that this is a good study strategy. Use the two strategies that researchers know work. Get in there and get the job done in the best possible way.

Of course you have to first take information in. You have to read the material enough to make sure you understand it. You want to build in enough repetition to make sure that you can get the information out again—remember it for the test. After some repetition, try to pull the information out by using a practice test. If you could not recall the information, give yourself some more repetition. Use more encoding strategies. Then practice test yourself again. When you successfully complete a practice test you will be ready for the real one. You might want to double-check by giving yourself that practice test again to make sure you can remember the material a week later or a month later, as necessary.

Do what works. Using the planner discussed in Week One, plan out several short sessions of studying. Those who got low grades looked for a several hour block of time near the test so they could cram. The winning strategy is to look for many short sessions when you can spend an hour or maybe 45 minutes reviewing the material, taking a practice test, or going through flash cards. Look for a few blocks of time where you and a classmate can meet briefly before or after class to quiz each other. Just sitting together and studying doesn't work. Test each other, talk about examples, or read each other's notes.

Just Do This!

Space out your studying. For example, rather than 2 three-hour cram sessions (total 6 hours) right before the test, spread these six hours out into 6 one-hour sessions. It will be easier on you *and* more effective. Use your planner as soon as a test is assigned to make this happen.

Also, you must practice test. There are many easy ways to do that. Here are some ways. Do as many as you can.

1. Look for practice tests or review questions at the end of the chapter. Many textbooks provide these and some have answers in the back of the book so you can test yourself.

2. Get a study partner and quiz each other.

3. Make your own flash cards.

4. Draw a line down the middle of a sheet of paper. Put the questions or vocabulary words on the left and the answers or definitions on the right. Fold the paper down the middle so you see only the questions. Write your answers on scratch paper. Check your answers. When you get a question right, put a check next to it on the left side of the question. After you get two check marks (you got it right twice), cross out that question and only study the ones you are still having difficulty with. That way your study sessions get shorter and you are focusing on the right material. Keep working until you get them all right. Then test yourself again on all the questions. Work until you get them all right on one trial.

Reflect and Connect:

Have you used these strategies? Since research has shown that they work, is there any reason why you would not use them from now on?

Checking in with my Brain	
THE MOST USEFUL THING I LEARNED IN THIS UNIT WAS:	
THE NEW STRATEGIES THAT I TRIED WERE:	
Strategy	How did it work for me?
WHAT WILL I KEEP DOING?	
WHAT PREVIOUS HABITS WILL I CHANGE?	
WHAT PROGRESS AM I MAKING?	

1. How much total time did you spend studying for the test?

   _____

2. About how many of those hours were spent the day before or on the day of the test and how many were spent on days other than the day before/on? _____

3. About how many days *before* the test did you begin studying for the test? _____

4. Out of those days, how many days did you actually study for the test? _____

5. How many repetitions of the material did you provide yourself in preparation for the test? _____

6. How much of the assigned textbook material for this test did you read?   ¼   ½   ¾   all

7. How many hours sleep did you get the night before the test? _____

8. How many times did you practice test for this test? _____

9. What memory strategies did you use to prepare for the test. Look at the chart of encoding strategies as a guideline to answer. _____

   _____

   _____

   _____

10. Did you take notes in class? Yes   No   If yes, how many times did you review them?_____

11. Did you go to a lab for extra help?_____

12. Did you use a study partner to prepare for the test? _____

13. How many days/classes did you miss during the time period of the last test to this test? _____

Zadina Model of Academic Memory Processes

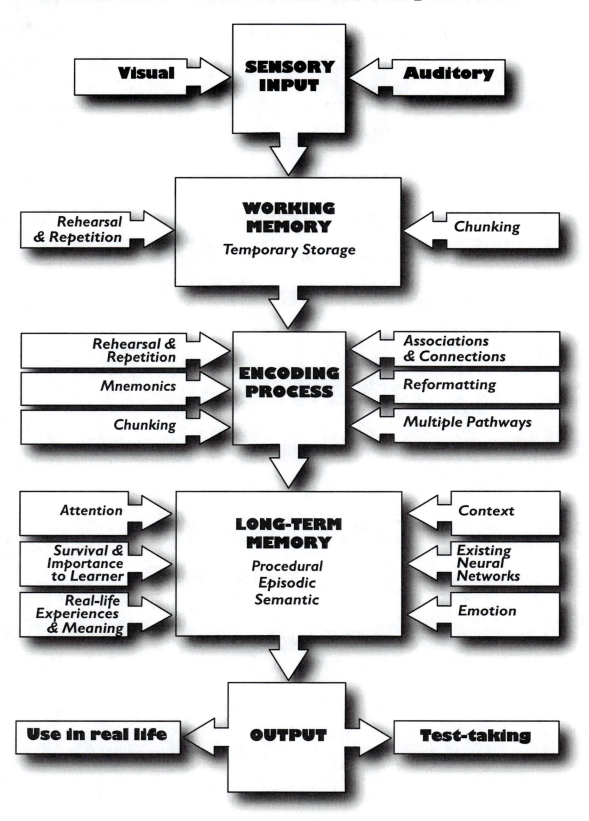

 SIX WEEKS TO A BRAIN UPGRADE

FIRE IT

Your Body and Learning

Let's see how you are doing right now. Write the number in the blank that best describes how you **usually** behave. Answer **honestly** so you can find out how to improve your brain.

5) always   4) most of the time   3) maybe   2) not very often   1) never

_____ 1. When I am studying and get tired, I push myself to keep going rather than going to bed or taking a nap.

_____ 2. I stay up late to study so I can cut out sleeping time to get more study time.

_____ 3. My schedule keeps me from getting enough sleep.

_____ 4. I have something sweet for breakfast, such as toaster tarts, sweet rolls, soft drinks, cereal with sugar, or a sweet granola bar.

_____ 5. I skip lunch or I get a snack, such as chips or candy.

_____ 6. I get lunch from a fast food restaurant (burgers, tacos, fried chicken, fries, soft drinks) during the week.

_____ 7. I sit for at least five hours a day.

_____ 8. I eat three vegetables a day.

_____ 9. I get aerobic exercise 3 times a week.

_____ 10. I walk 30 minutes a day (or a total of 2 ½ hours a week).

_____ 11. I work out in the gym or work with weights at least 45 minutes a week.

_____ 12. I participate in sports or dancing at least twice a week.

_____ 13. I study out loud with a friend through discussions or quizzing each other.

_____ 14. I partner with other students to figure out material or to explain it to each other.

To calculate your score, do these steps.

1. For items 8–14, reverse the score:
   a. If you have a 5, change to 1
   b. If you have a 4, change to 2
   c. If you have a 3 it stays the same
   d. If you have a 2, change to 4
   e. If you have a 1, change to 5

2. Add your scores

3. If your score is 56–70 you will benefit greatly from this week. If you can make the changes suggested and keep the habits for several weeks, you should see a big improvement. Even if you can't keep these new habits every day, the more you do, the better care you are taking of your brain and the better it will work for you.

4. If your score is 28–55 you have room for improvement. Make the changes suggested in this chapter as often as you can, and you will get more brain power from your brain and keep it healthier.

5. If your score is 14–27, congratulations. Keep up the great work! Read the chapter carefully and see where you can make more improvements.

The Research

Scientists know for a fact that sleep is linked to a better brain and better learning. Researchers Mary Carskadon and Bill Dement found that teenagers actually need more sleep than young children or adults because their brains are going through an important growth stage. Teenagers also find it hard to go to bed early and need to sleep late in the morning because their sleep cycles are different.

Researcher Jessica Payne and her lab found that people would forget information during a busy day but sleep would strengthen the memories.

Other research showed that getting sleep was more helpful in getting good grades than additional study time. Neuroscientist Clifford Saper suggests "learn, sleep, repeat."

Learn, sleep, repeat!

So What?

Sleep on it! Since we know that sleep is associated with a better brain and better learning, then you need to act on this information. The best time to study is before you go to sleep. Another way to use this information is to take a brief nap after you study for a while. This doesn't mean that you don't have to study, but it means that sleep is a necessary part of the learning process and sometimes you are better off sleeping than forcing yourself to study for a longer period of time. If you have spaced out your studying over days or weeks, sleeping the night before a test may be better than staying up late to study. Avoid early morning schedules for work or classes if you can. If not, then catch up on your late morning sleep on the weekends or days off.

Just Do This!

Try taking a 20 minute nap after you study for a while. Longer than 20 minutes may make you groggy when you get up, but after 20 minutes you should be able to start studying again with a refreshed brain. Try to review material every night before you go to sleep. Set aside that time. Make it a habit. Be sure to get 8 hours of sleep the night before a test.

Reflect and Connect:

How can this information make a difference to you?

The Research:

Scientists looked at the diets of middle school students. They found that those who ate a sugary breakfast (pastries, soft drinks, sugared cereal, candy) performed on tests of memory and attention at the level of a 70 year old! (not a good thing!). This would apply to all ages. However, eating a breakfast with protein (eggs, beans on toast, pizza, and sandwiches) improved their ability to learn and remember. Of course, this applies to lunch as well.

Scientists in Ohio found that students who were dehydrated (had not had enough water) did not perform as well as students who were not.

What you eat affects your brain!

So What?

You are what you eat! And since your brain is only about 3% of your body weight but consumes about 20% of your body's fuel, what you eat really affects your brain health and how well you learn. The brain needs fuel throughout the day. If you were working out in a gym to build muscles, you would know that you would have to replenish your body's energy through eating. The same applies to working your brain hard. Sugar gives a quick boost of energy, but then your blood sugar drops and you feel even worse than before you ate the sugar. Blood sugar surges and drops are bad for your brain.

If what you eat affects your brain and how you learn, then you need to accept responsibility for that. You know the saying "garbage in, garbage out" usually applies to computers but it applies to your brain as well. You have to keep your brain fueled throughout the day. Unfortunately, most food available in vending machines is bad for your brain. You may have to bring food to school or if you can't, make the best possible choices. Good choices are nuts, berries, yogurt, fruit, dark chocolate, and pumpkin seeds. Drink water, tea, or coffee. Other good brain foods are salmon, tuna, sardines, leafy greens, broccoli, cauliflower, cabbage, avocado, eggs, and beans.

Just Do This!

Think about your food choices, plan ahead, and eat what makes you smarter!

Reflect and Connect:

Now that you know what foods fuel your brain, how will it affect your food choices?

The Research:

Exercise makes a better brain. Neuroscientist Cyrus Raji found that people who engaged in more physical activity had more gray matter in their brains in areas important to learning and memory. Do you have trouble remembering? Bernward (yes this is correct spelling) Winter discovered that just 3 minutes of aerobic exercise improved short and long term memory. Researcher Charles Hillman found a relationship between how much physical activity a student did and how well they did in school, including on standardized tests. John Ratey did an experiment that had some students doing exercise before school and found that their grades went up. The better they did on the physical tests he gave them, the better they scored on achievement tests.

If you sit for 20 minutes, you start producing hormones with a negative effect on the brain.

> No drug can have the same effect on the brain as exercise.

So What?

This research is well-documented. It means that you are going to have to get up and move around! Move as much as possible during the day. It means you must plan for physical activity, just as you plan to eat, sleep, study, and work. Neuroscientist Cyrus Raji makes a strong statement about the link between exercise and the brain. He says that there is no drug that can have the same effect on the brain as exercise.

Just Do This!

Exercise may be one of the best things that you can do to improve your brain and it can be fun. Exercise can be dancing or sports or bicycling. Pick something you like and use it to rest your mind while you make it stronger.

Get that 3 minutes of aerobic exercise before a test by walking around the building really quickly if possible. Do as many toe lifts (standing on your toes up and down) as possible (hide in the restroom if need be).

Try to stand up every 20 minutes if you can. Experiment with studying standing up, such as at a counter. You may find you get more learning in less time. When you are studying, set the timer for 45 minutes and then use the next 15 minutes to do something active, but brief, such as walking the dog, taking out the trash, emptying the dishwasher or dryer, shooting a few hoops, taking a walk around the block, or anything that gets you up and moving. You could dribble a basketball while you are reciting things from memory. You can play pitch and catch while quizzing a friend. Record a class lecture and listen to it while you ride your bike or walk.

Reflect and Connect:

What does this information mean to you? How will it affect your behavior?

The Research:

It has been known for a very long time that the best way to learn something is to teach someone else. This activates all of the brain pathways and most of the strategies that you have learned. When you teach something, you first have to have read and understood it. Then you have to think about it and how you would explain it. You speak when you teach and sometimes you may write out your ideas. You have to recall the information and reassemble it in order to speak about it. You elaborate on it and think of examples. You can teach another student or you could teach by creating a blog, a wiki, or a FAQ. Get a free account at http://wordpress.com/ .

> By helping others, you also help yourself!

Another way to take advantage of the social brain is to have a study partner or partners because each person is bringing their existing neural network to the experience, providing a stronger background from which to approach the new material. In addition, being social is pleasurable to the brain and when you are more positive, you learn better.

So What?

This supports the idea that when you help others, you also help yourself. Benefits of teaching others:

- You gain a deeper understanding
- You review the material again yourself as you teach it
- You can picture yourself explaining it when you try to recall it on the test
- You incorporate many senses and multiple pathways
- You create a stronger neural network
- You realize what you don't understand before the test

Benefits of studying with a partner or in groups:

- They may be better able to see your missing pieces in your neural network – why you don't understand – than the teacher who has such a developed network
- You can do the most important strategy of self-testing by testing each other
- You can turn flashcards into games and challenges
- You can make funny faces or jokes with answers that might help you remember them better
- It reduces stress and anxiety

Just Do This!

Include studying with others as part of your long-term test study process. Pretend you are the instructor and teach them.

Reflect and Connect:

How have you used your social brain to make learning better? What can you do differently?

If you have applied what you have learned, the only way you can go is up! Take the quiz on the last page of this book to see how much progress you have made so far.

Study skills are necessary, but not sufficient—they are not enough. The most important factor is motivation, and that can only come from you. How do you get motivation? Set a goal. When someone really wants to get something, do something, accomplish something, they find a way! You know that. Why doesn't it apply to school? You may not be pushing yourself to succeed because your goals are either too vague, too far away from now, or seemingly unrelated to your school work or you think that the goal is a grade in a course. But let's rethink this.

Grades are not the goal. Yes, you heard me right. **It's learning that's important!** So let's forget about grades as a goal. Good grades come from *another* goal—they are a byproduct. When you have a bigger goal in mind, you work hard and you get good grades.

You may not know what kind of a career you want. You may be drifting along without direction so the courses do not matter to you. You are just getting through them. But do you want a great life? Do you want a good income, to be a good parent, and to make good decisions? Then your goal is to have a great brain—an *educated brain* with good thinking skills.

Education grows that brain. Any course you take will contribute to you eventually having a better life if you throw yourself into it because as you learn, you change your brain. You become a better thinker. This pays off in future courses and in your job and family life. Throw yourself into every course and apply what you learned here. Set the goal of a better life. Then once you find your passion and what you want to do, you will have the brain to get you to that goal.

We are right back to the first week in this workbook: all about what is in *your* head. Take control of your brain. Set your intentions. Believe in yourself. Realize that it isn't that you *can't,* but that you *haven't* grown the neural networks **yet**. Use all your senses. Control your emotions. Enjoy the feel-good chemicals from working hard. Take charge! Know that self-regulation is a key to a good life. Think about your thinking. Control your attention. Use specific strategies that work for you! Use the strategies that scientists know **work**! Don't waste your time. Create a lifestyle that will get you to your goals by taking care of your brain with sleep, diet, and exercise. Learn from others and help others along the way.

You can change your brain and become smarter. It will take some time and effort but will serve you well not in one course, one semester, one degree, but for the rest of your life. You know what to do.

Just Do It!

WIRE IT

1. Using your planner, write in two 20-minute nap sessions in your two largest study blocks of time.

2. Using your planner, block off the last 20 minutes before you go to sleep for a review of the day's material.

3. One thing I could eliminate to get more nap or sleep time would be to reduce the time I spend:

_____

4. Two healthier foods I could eat for breakfast instead of what I currently eat are:

   a. _____

   b _____

5. Two healthier foods I could usually eat at lunch instead of my current choices are:

   a. _____

   b _____

6. Two foods I could bring to school and eat on break are:

   a. _____

   b _____

7. Two ways I could move while studying:

   a. _____

   b. _____

8. I could work 15 minutes of physical activity into my daily schedule by (one idea- park your car farther from the classroom building) _____

9. Three ways I could include more physical activity into my week:

   a. _____

   b _____

   c. _____

10. One way I could study with a friend would be to (describe content and what you would do, such as make up multiplication math problems for each other to practice test):

_____

_____

_____

TOPIC   **DATE**

Drawings, Study Questions...

✓ Make drawings and sketches here later as you go through your notes or if you get time during note-taking
✓ If the teacher says "I forgot to mention" and backs up, you can write it next to the relevant material and draw an arrow
✓ As you study your notes, you can pull out important words or facts and write them here
✓ Turn the notes into questions and use them to study

Take Notes Here

✓ Spread them out so you can picture them later
✓ Only write down what might be on the test or is important to know: don't try to write everything
✓ Keep them brief
✓ Print—easier to read and recall than cursive
✓ Keep another color of ink handy to make something stand out
✓ Abbreviate – create your own symbols
   T = Test – Teacher says will be on test
   M = Memorize
   ? = Not sure – look this up
   Sp? = might not be spelled right

Write anything special here: something to be sure to do when you study; reminder of something you know will be on the test

Follow Up: to do, find out, or ask

Assignment Plan

Course	Date	Assignment	Date Due	When	Where	✓

A.2—How in Charge Are You?

Write the number in the blank that best describes how you **usually** behave.
Answer **honestly** so you can find out how to improve your brain.

5) always   4) most of the time   3) maybe   2) not very often   1) never

_____   1. I control my anxiety or nervousness on tests.

_____   2. I believe that I can succeed in this course if I work hard enough.

_____   3. I believe that hard work is more important than natural talent at something.

_____   4. I am able to control distracting or upsetting thoughts.

_____   5. I draw pictures to help me remember.

_____   6. I ask myself questions about the material before and while I read.

_____   7. I believe that you can change the IQ (intelligence) you were born with.

_____   8. I test myself on the material.

_____   9. I think of how what I already know relates to the material that is new.

_____   10. I look up information to understand new material better.

_____   11. I think about how well I understand material and back up if necessary.

_____   12. I make notes on what I don't understand and get it explained.

_____   13. I plan my schedule for doing assignments in a planner.

_____   14. I am organized.

_____   15. I control my emotions.

_____   16. I study my wrong answers to figure out why I missed them.

_____   17. I have a system for taking notes.

_____   18. I have several ways to make information easier to remember.

_____   19. I can control my attention in class.

_____   20. I get 8 hours of sleep a night and/or I take naps.

_____   21. I avoid studying right before a test.

_____   22. I use more than one sense when learning: seeing, hearing, speaking, or writing.

_____   23. I study with other students outside of class.

_____   24. I turn assignments in on time.

_____   25. I am happy with the grades that I have been making.

How are you doing now? Add your points and check your score:

100+   You are doing well! Improve where you can and help other students. You will get even better!

51–99   You will benefit greatly from doing the activities in this book. Do all of them, add new habits, and experience better learning!

0–50   You **can** change your brain and raise this score. Devote yourself wholeheartedly to this book. Keep doing all the new strategies that you learn, adding to your skills and habits. Watch other students and learn from their skills. You will make progress and see results!

Now compare the score on the one you just took with the quiz on page 8. Did you improve? If you did, congratulations! You changed your brain and made yourself smarter. If you didn't, then we have to ask, how much did you take control of your brain? Did you try most of the ideas? How much effort did you put forth? Go back to the beginning and do it all again. Only you can change your brain.